MiNi MaKeRs

mini
WEARABLES

by Rebecca Felix

Summit Free Public Library

Lerner Publications / Minneapolis

Lerner Publications Company
A division of Lerner Publishing Group, Inc.
241 First Avenue North
Minneapolis, MN 55401 USA

For reading levels and more information, look up this title at www.lernerbooks.com.

Main body text set in Bembo STD 16/25.
Typeface provided by Monotype Typography.

Library of Congress Cataloging-in-Publication Data

Names: Felix, Rebecca, 1984- author.
Title: Mini wearables / by Rebecca Felix.
Description: Minneapolis : Lerner Publications, [2016] | Series: Mini makers | Audience: Ages 7-11. | Audience: Grades 4 to 6. | Includes bibliographical references and index.
Identifiers: LCCN 2016018650 (print) | LCCN 2016020017 (ebook) | ISBN 9781512426359 (lb : alk. paper) | ISBN 9781512428131 (eb pdf)
Subjects: LCSH: Miniature craft–Juvenile literature. | Costume jewelry–Juvenile literature. | Dress accessories–Juvenile literature. | CYAC: Handicraft.
Classification: LCC TT212 .F45 2016 (print) | LCC TT212 (ebook) | DDC 745.594/2–dc23

LC record available at https://lccn.loc.gov/2016018650

Manufactured in the United States of America
1-41407-23327-8/4/2016

Photo Acknowledgements
The images in this book are used with the permission of: © Mighty Media, Inc., pp. 4, 5 (bottom), 8 (left), 8 (right), 9, 10, 11 (top), 11 (middle), 11 (bottom), 12, 13 (top), 13 (middle), 13 (bottom), 14, 15 (top), 15 (middle), 15 (bottom), 16, 17 (top), 17 (middle), 17 (bottom), 18, 19 (top), 19 (middle), 19 (bottom), 20, 21 (top), 21 (middle), 21 (bottom), 22, 22 (felt), 23 (top), 23 (middle), 23 (bottom), 24, 25 (top), 25 (middle), 25 (bottom), 26, 27 (top), 27 (middle), 27 (bottom), 28 (top), 28 (middle), 28 (bottom), 29; © Ingvar Bjork/Shutterstock Images, p. 4 (scissors); © Monkey Business Images/Shutterstock Images, p. 5 (top); © Michael Dechev/Shutterstock Images, p. 5 (markers); © Lane V. Erickson/Shutterstock Images, p. 6; © Photographee.eu/Shutterstock Images, p. 7; © Oleksandr Kostiuchenko/Shutterstock Images, p. 8 (needle); © Vladvm/Shutterstock Images, p. 8 (paintbrush); © sarkao/Shutterstock Images, p. 9 (googly eyes); © kozirsky/Shutterstock Images, p. 9 (paints); © Africa Studio/Shutterstock Images, 9 (ribbon); © NotWithClaws/Shutterstock Images, p. 13 (bottles); © STILLFX/Shutterstock Images, p. 14 (ribbon).

Front cover: © Mighty Media, Inc.

Back cover: © Mighty Media, Inc. (left, right); © kemalbas/iStockphoto (buttons); © Ryan Lindberg/iStockphoto (scissors).

CONTENTS

Getting Started ~~~~~~~~~~~~~~~~~~~~~~~~~~~~~~~~~ 4

Before You Begin ~~~~~~~~~~~~~~~~~~~~~~~~~~~~~~~~ 6

Bite-Sized Beast Clips ~~~~~~~~~~~~~~~~~~~~~~~~~~ 10

Bitty Bottle Necklace ~~~~~~~~~~~~~~~~~~~~~~~~~~~ 12

Pint-Sized Bow Tie ~~~~~~~~~~~~~~~~~~~~~~~~~~~~~~ 14

Super-Small Ball Bracelet ~~~~~~~~~~~~~~~~~~~~~~~ 16

Mini Nest Necklace ~~~~~~~~~~~~~~~~~~~~~~~~~~~~~~ 18

Petite Dominoes Bracelet ~~~~~~~~~~~~~~~~~~~~~~~~ 20

Itsy-Bitsy Bloom Band ~~~~~~~~~~~~~~~~~~~~~~~~~~~ 22

Teeny Top Hat ~~~~~~~~~~~~~~~~~~~~~~~~~~~~~~~~~~~ 24

Wee Book Key Chain ~~~~~~~~~~~~~~~~~~~~~~~~~~~~~~ 26

Wrapping Up ~~~~~~~~~~~~~~~~~~~~~~~~~~~~~~~~~~~~~ 30

Glossary ~~~~~~ 31

Further Information ~~~~~~~~~~~~~~~~~~~~~~~~~~~~~ 31

Index ~~~~~~ 32

WEE WEARABLES

Have you ever wished you could add a wee bit of flair to your favorite outfit? Do you want to show off your style in small doses? Big bows, huge hats, and giant jewelry can sometimes be too much. Mini wearables add a more delicate, **subtle** touch. And these **diminutive adornments** are just plain fun too!

Picture wearing a top hat no taller than a thimble. Imagine a **petite**, pea-sized flower perched in your hair. These itty-bitty **embellishments** will **infuse** your outfits and accessories with fun. Break out your smallest supplies and teeniest tools. Prepare to make tiny wearable projects that make big statements!

Before You Begin
SLOW AND STEADY

Crafting tiny wearables can be challenging. Teeny parts can be hard to hold on to. The slightest breeze can send little pieces scattering. It can be tricky to work with minute materials. Super-small tools, such as toothpicks or tweezers, can make tiny tasks easier.

Before you kick off any new craft project, gather all the materials you will need. Many of the materials for mini wearables can be found at craft stores. An adult can also help you order materials online. Take the time to create a clean workspace before you begin crafting. Good lighting will help you keep an eye on small parts and pieces. Use small containers to keep track of your materials. Most importantly, work slowly and carefully. Your wee wearables will turn out best when you take your time making them. Patience is your most important tool when crafting.

Work Safely!

Some crafts require the use of sharp or hot tools. That means they also require adult help. An adult will make sure your fingers, eyes, and workspace are protected as you craft amazing mini creations.

IMAGINATION
and Fashion

Making mini wearables can be challenging. But it should also be fun! As you create tiny ties, mini charms, and more, get creative. Think about what you could add to your tiny creations to make them special. Maybe you could use different materials, several colors, or add small gems. Go for it! Any small detail you can dream up will help make your mini creations your own.

You can also get creative with the tools you use. Find small everyday items that can help you make your mini masterpieces more easily. Figure out new ways to fasten tiny things to your clothing. Use your imagination, and have fun!

BITE-SIZED BEAST CLIPS

Create teensy creatures to bite your backpack, belt loops, or shoelaces!

MATERIALS

- newspaper
- mini spring clothespins
- paint
- paintbrushes
- paint pens
- craft foam
- scissors
- pipe cleaners
- all-purpose glue
- assorted googly eyes

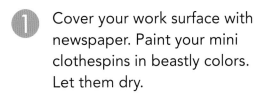

1. Cover your work surface with newspaper. Paint your mini clothespins in beastly colors. Let them dry.

2. Use the paint pens to decorate your clothespins with stripes, dots, and other monstrous patterns.

3. Next create some body parts. Cut tiny hands, feet, and monster heads from the craft foam. Leave a small stem on each head to glue to the inside of the clothespin.

4. Cut a pipe cleaner for arms or legs. Thread a pipe cleaner through the spring on a clothespin. Repeat using the rest of the clothespins.

5. Glue the feet or hands onto the ends of the pipe cleaner. Repeat for the rest of the monsters.

6. Now bring your bitty beasts to life. Glue on googly eyes. Give your beasts as many eyes as you want! Let the glue dry. Then clip your mini monsters to your clothing, backpack, shoes, and more for some beastly fun!

BITTY BOTTLE NECKLACE

Turn a teeny bottle holding a microscopic collection into a mini necklace charm!

MATERIALS
- tiny bottle with cork
- headpin
- wire cutters
- round-nose pliers
- items to put inside the bottle, such as sand, candy sprinkles, a tiny slip of paper with a message, pebbles, and more
- strong, quick-setting glue
- leather cord
- scissors

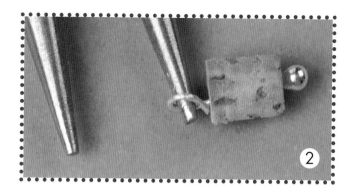

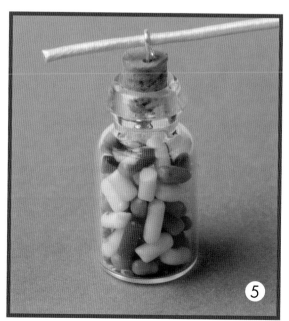

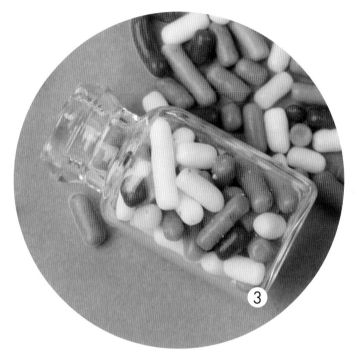

1. Remove the cork from the bottle. Push the headpin up from the bottom of the cork through to the top.

2. Trim the **excess** headpin, leaving enough to make a small loop. Use the pliers to form the small loop with the remaining pin.

3. Fill the bottle with tiny objects and materials.

4. Use glue to secure the cork back in the bottle.

5. Cut the leather cord to your desired necklace length. Thread the cord through the headpin loop, and tie the ends together to form a necklace chain.

6. Show off your neat little necklace and its tiny treasures!

PINT-SIZED BOW TIE

Attach a dash of class with a bitty bow-tie pin no bigger than a button!

MATERIALS

- ⅝-inch (1.6 centimeter) wide ribbon
- ruler or tape measure
- scissors
- small binder clip
- thread
- ¼-inch (0.6 cm) wide ribbon
- hot glue gun and glue sticks
- pin back

1. Cut a 3-inch (7.6 cm) piece of the ⅝-inch (1.6 cm) wide ribbon. Lay the ribbon face down, with the long edge on the bottom. Fold the left end over to meet the right end. Now fold both ends to the left to meet the first fold. Turn over.

2. Pinch the ribbon in the middle so the top and bottom edges come together.

3. Secure with a binder clip, and arrange the folded ribbon to look like a bow tie.

4. Wrap the center of the bow tie with a short piece of thread. Then remove the binder clip.

5. Cut a 1-inch (2.5 cm) piece of the ¼-inch (0.6 cm) wide ribbon. Wrap the ribbon around the middle of the bow tie, over the thread. With an adult's help, glue the ribbon in place.

6. Attach the bow tie to the pin back with hot glue. Let the glue dry. Sport your teeny-tiny tie next time you need a wee bit of **elegance**!

SUPER-SMALL BALL BRACELET

Decorate teensy sports balls to make a sporty bracelet.

MATERIALS

- newspaper
- 40–60 round beads in two different sizes
- wooden skewer
- plastic cup
- paint in several colors, including orange, white, green, and yellow
- paintbrushes
- fine-point permanent markers
- bracelet memory wire
- wire cutters
- round-nose pliers
- 2 tiny beads

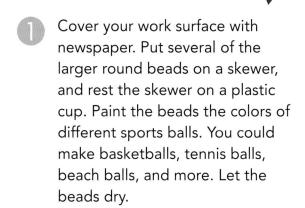

1. Cover your work surface with newspaper. Put several of the larger round beads on a skewer, and rest the skewer on a plastic cup. Paint the beads the colors of different sports balls. You could make basketballs, tennis balls, beach balls, and more. Let the beads dry.

2. Use the permanent markers to add details to the balls. Draw black lines around the orange beads to look like basketballs. Draw dotted red lines around the white beads to look like stitching on baseballs.

3. Cut a length of memory wire to the size you want the bracelet to be. Use the round-nose pliers to make a small loop on one end.

4. Thread the beads onto the wire. Start with a tiny bead. Then alternate plain beads with the beads you decorated. Create a pattern.

5. Once the bracelet is filled, add the other tiny bead. Cut off any excess wire, but leave a little bit at the end. Use the pliers to form a loop with this bit of wire.

6. Now shape the bead-covered wire to fit your wrist. Wear your bitty ball bracelet at the next sporting event you go to!

MINI NEST NECKLACE

Carry baby bird eggs everywhere in an itsy-bitsy bird's nest necklace!

MATERIALS

- air-dry clay
- newspaper
- paint
- paintbrush
- strong, quick-setting glue
- 2 jewelry bails
- thimble
- moss
- tweezers
- jewelry chain
- wire cutters
- needle-nose pliers
- 2 jump rings

1. Shape small balls of clay into ovals. They should look like tiny eggs. Let them dry. Then cover your work surface with newspaper, and paint the eggs.

2. Glue the jewelry bails to opposite sides of the thimble.

3. Ball up the moss to form a tiny nest. Glue the nest into the thimble.

4. Glue the painted eggs into the nest. Use the tweezers to place the eggs in the nest.

5. Cut the chain to the length you want. Make sure the necklace will fit over your head.

6. Use the pliers to open a jump ring. Attach the ring to one end of the chain and a jewelry bail, and close the ring. Repeat on the other side. Wear your little nest for a bit of springtime style wherever you go!

Tiny Tip!

Jewelry bails are used to attach **pendants** to necklace chains. Jump rings are small wire rings that can be opened and closed. Both bails and jump rings can be found at most craft stores.

PETITE DOMINOES BRACELET

Fold a fun bracelet, and decorate it to look like little dominoes!

MATERIALS

- white paper
- ruler
- pencil
- scissors
- fine-tipped colored markers

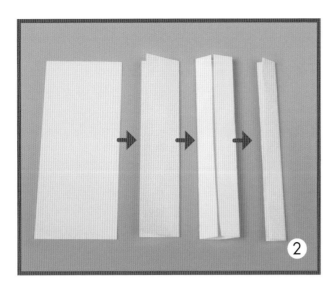

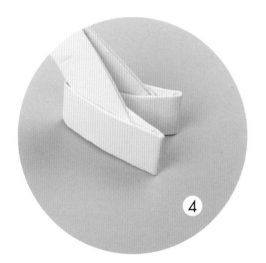

1. Use the ruler and pencil to measure and mark twenty to twenty-six strips on the paper. Each strip should be 3½ inches (8.9 cm) long and 1½ inches (3.8 cm) wide. Cut out the strips.

2. Fold a strip in half the long way. Open and fold the sides to the center crease. Fold in half the long way one more time.

3. Fold the strip in half the short way. Open and fold so the short ends meet at the middle crease. Repeat with the remaining strips.

4. Push the two ends of one folded strip through the loops of another folded strip to make a V. Repeat, attaching the folded strips together. Stop when your bracelet is the correct length for you to slip over your wrist.

5. Use colored markers to decorate each piece of the bracelet to look like a different domino.

6. Connect your bracelet by unfolding one of the end pieces so the flaps are extra long. Slide the long flaps into one of the slots of the other end of the bracelet. Then fold both ends and slip them back into the other slot. Your dynamite domino bracelet is ready to wear at game night!

ITSY-BITSY BLOOM BAND

Create a hair band using button-sized bunches of petite petals!

MATERIALS

- green floral wire
- scissors
- ruler
- 26-gauge green wire
- felt in several colors
- all-purpose glue
- pin
- beads

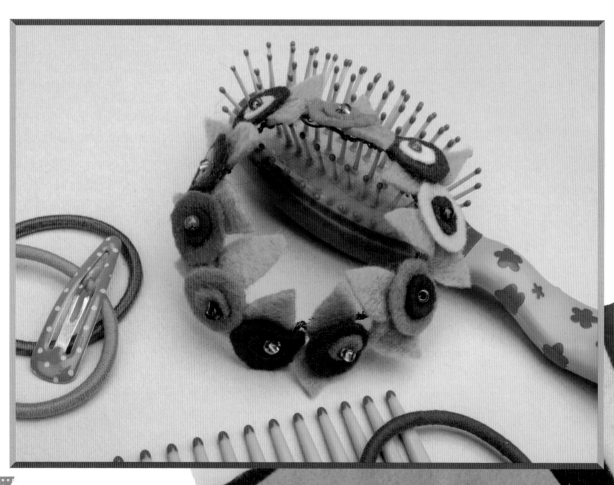

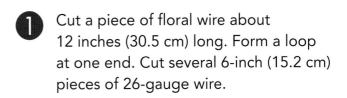

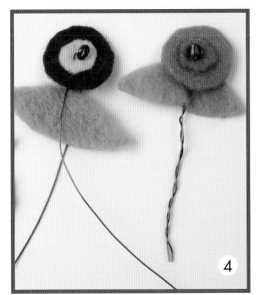

1. Cut a piece of floral wire about 12 inches (30.5 cm) long. Form a loop at one end. Cut several 6-inch (15.2 cm) pieces of 26-gauge wire.

2. Cut several small circles out of felt. Cut smaller circles in contrasting colors. Then, cut leaf-shaped green felt pieces.

3. Glue a small circle in the center of a larger circle. Use a pin to make two small holes in the center. Push a piece of 26-gauge wire partway through one of the holes. Thread a bead onto the wire where it meets the felt. Push the wire through the other hole. Twist the wire at the back.

4. Place a leaf-shaped piece of felt at the base of the flower between the two wires. Twist the wires around the middle of the felt to secure in place.

5. Place the flower next to the loop in the floral wire. Wrap the stem around the floral wire to secure in place.

6. Repeat steps 3 through 5 to complete your **garland**. Wrap the garland around a ponytail or bun. Thread the end of the floral wire through the loop, and twist to secure. Show off your fun floral fashion!

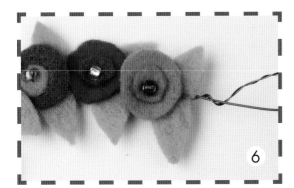

Tiny Tip!

To create perfect circles, trace circular object, such as coins.

TEENY TOP HAT

Turn a little lid or cap into a tiny top hat.
Add mini details to give it a theme!

MATERIALS

- cardboard
- circular object to trace (slightly larger than the cap)
- pencil
- scissors
- newspaper
- paint
- paintbrushes
- plastic cylindrical cap
- needle
- 12 inches (30.5 cm) of elastic string
- all-purpose glue
- pipe cleaner
- feather, mini pom-pom, ribbon, and other materials for decorating the hat

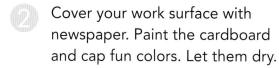

1. Trace and cut out a cardboard circle. Make sure it has a larger **circumference** than the plastic cap.

2. Cover your work surface with newspaper. Paint the cardboard and cap fun colors. Let them dry.

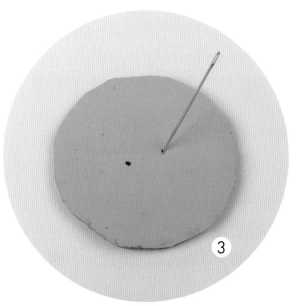

3. Use a needle to poke two holes through the center of the cardboard. Push the elastic string ends up through the holes. Knot both ends of the string at the point where the elastic is tight enough to hold the hat in on your head, but not too tight. Secure the knots with glue.

4. Glue a piece of pipe cleaner to the edge of the cardboard circle. Trim any excess pipe cleaner.

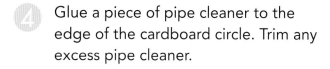

5. Glue the cap to the middle of the cardboard. It should cover up the knots of string.

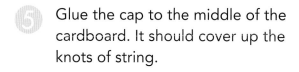

6. Glue a feather to the side of the cap. Then glue a pom-pom to the top. Cut a piece of ribbon long enough to wrap around the cap. This will be the hat band. Wrap the ribbon around the hat, just above the brim, and glue in place. Wear your little hat to show off your super-small fashion sense!

WEE BOOK KEY CHAIN

Craft a bitty book that you can actually write in! Hang it anywhere you need to leave a little note.

MATERIALS

- thin cardboard
- ruler
- pencil
- scissors
- ballpoint pen
- plain paper
- scrap cardboard
- pushpin
- needle
- white thread
- decorative paper
- glue stick
- key ring

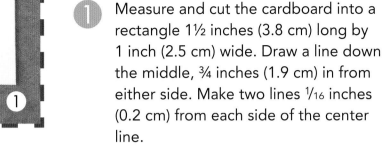

1. Measure and cut the cardboard into a rectangle 1½ inches (3.8 cm) long by 1 inch (2.5 cm) wide. Draw a line down the middle, ¾ inches (1.9 cm) in from either side. Make two lines 1/16 inches (0.2 cm) from each side of the center line.

2. Use a ballpoint pen to **score** the two outer marks on each piece. Fold the scored lines to form the spine of your book.

3. Cut eight pieces of plain paper to 1¼ inches (3.2 cm) wide by 7/8 inches (2.2 cm) long. Stack the pieces, and fold the stack in half. Trim the edges if needed to make them even. These are your book's pages.

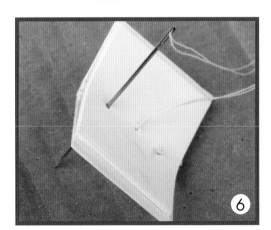

4. Place the cardboard rectangle on the scrap cardboard. Center the pages on the rectangle.

5. Use a pushpin to make three evenly spaced holes that go through the center of the pages and the cardboard.

6. Thread the needle. Pull it through the top hole of the pages and the cover. Stitch up through the center hole and down through the bottom hole. Repeat to **reinforce** the stitches. Tie a knot after the last stitch, and cut off any excess thread.

Tiny Tip!

To thread the needle, poke the thread through the tiny hole at the needle's end. Pull the thread through until the thread is the length you want it.

Wee Book Key Chain continued next page

7 Cut a piece of decorative paper 2½ inches (6.4 cm) long and 2 inches (5 cm) wide. Place the paper face down, and center your book on it. Use the pen to draw around the edges of the book cover.

8 Cut off the corners of the decorative paper. To form flaps, cut at an angle from the edge to each corner.

9 Center the book back on the paper. Cut a V-shaped notch on both the top and bottom of the paper, just above and below the book's spine.

10 Place the decorative paper face down. Spread a layer of glue within the rectangle. Set the book on the glue, and press to secure.

11 Put glue on the top and bottom flaps. Press them onto the inside of the cover. Repeat with the side flaps.

12 Thread the needle, knot the thread, and run it between the pages and the cover just under the top stitch. Tie into a loop and trim off any excess thread. Use this loop to hook the mini book onto your key ring!

Show Off Your Wee Wearables!

Finding cool ways to display your tiny crafts makes them seem even more amazing! Show off how small your wearables really are. Attach your wee book key chains to a jacket zipper or backpack. The bigger the jacket or backpack, the smaller your bitty books will seem.

Wrapping Up

CLEANUP AND SAFEKEEPING

Now that you have finished crafting, cleanup is the next step. Put away all the tiny tools you used. Pick up every teeny piece and part that is left over from your work. Store small items in little tins, containers, or plastic bags.

When cleanup is complete, find a safe place to display your creations! You will want to make sure you keep your items in a safe and handy spot so that you can wear them again and again. Keep delicate creations in small boxes or drawer compartments so they don't get crushed. Be sure to keep your tiny crafts out of reach of younger siblings and pets who might swallow the petite projects!

Keep Crafting!

Get inspired by your wearable works of art. Dream up new ideas for tiny accessories. Or make your own versions of the mini crafts you constructed. Think big and create small!

GLOSSARY

adornments: things worn to make a person or object more attractive

circumference: the distance around the outer edge of a circle

diminutive: very small

elegance: gracefulness or stylishness

embellishments: things added to objects to make them more beautiful

excess: extra or more than is needed

garland: a wreath or string with materials, such as leaves or flowers, that can be used as decoration

infuse: to add to or blend with something

pendants: hanging ornaments often worn on necklaces

petite: small or trim

reinforce: strengthen

score: to mark with grooves or lines

subtle: not easily noticed

Further Information

10 DIY Jewelry Projects for Kids
http://kidsactivitiesblog.com/49160/diy-jewelry-projects
This website is full of fun and easy jewelry projects that will let you show off your style in a big way.

Berne, Emma Carlson. *Jewelry Tips & Tricks.* Minneapolis: Lerner Publications, 2016.
This book is full of handy advice for making your own jewelry.

Kids' Accessories
http://www.marthastewart.com/275294/kids-accessories
Learn how to design and create your very own accessories.

Levete, Sarah. *Maker Projects for Kids Who Love Fashion.* New York: Crabtree Publishing Company, 2016.
Learn the basic design and crafting techniques you need to become a fashion designer.

INDEX

ball bracelet, 16–17

beast clips, 10–11

bloom band, 22–23

book key chain, 26–28, 29

bottle necklace, 12–13

bow tie, 14–15

cleaning up, 30

displaying projects, 29, 30

dominoes bracelet, 20, 21

getting started, 4–9

materials, 5, 6, 10, 12, 14, 16, 18, 20, 22, 24, 26, 30

nest necklace, 18–19

safety, 7

storage, 30

tools, 5, 6, 7, 9, 30

top hat, 5, 24–25

workspace, 6, 7, 11, 17, 19, 25